BRIAN JOHNSTON

Does Anyone Know Why We're Here?

Answers from Ecclesiastes

This book was professionally typeset on Reedsy.
Find out more at reedsy.com

Contents

1

CAN IT BE THAT EVERYTHING IS MEANINGLESS?

Ravi Zacharias, a Christian apologist, was once speaking to a large college crowd in the Philippines when he was suddenly interrupted. A student stood up and yelled, "Everything is meaningless!" Zacharias responded, "You don't believe that." The student yelled back, "Yes, I do!" "No, you don't." "I most certainly do. Who are you to tell me I don't?" "Then repeat your statement for me." "Everything is meaningless!" Ravi then said, "Please remain standing; this will only take a moment. I assume that you assume that your statement is meaningful. If your statement is meaningful, then everything is not meaningless. On the other hand, if everything is meaningless, then what you have just said is meaningless too. So, in effect, you have said nothing. You can sit down."

That young student was a sceptic, and I understand the above conversation was continued in private and he became a Christian. The consideration of whether it could be true that everything is meaningless is not a consideration we expect to find arising from within a biblical worldview. For in that Biblical worldview, God is accepted as existing and giving meaning and purpose to human existence. But the curious thing – at least at first sight – is that one entire book in the Bible is devoted to exploring whether or not everything is meaningless. Why should this be the case?

It's written by someone who doesn't fully identify himself, but rather enigmatically refers to himself by a term that translates as an academic or religious leader of assembly. Someone has not too inaccurately perhaps dubbed him as 'the Professor.' He does seem to have royal credentials and many consider this to be king Solomon's way of self-referencing. That the writer was a wise man goes without saying and his skill in learning is on display as he presents to us his thesis in the course of the 12 chapters that make up this potentially quite disconcerting book in the Bible. I say 'disconcerting' because the stance he takes is a rather sceptical one, and not one you might expect in the Bible. Why is this? Even a skim read through the book will provide a big clue as to what's going on. Many people have noticed it – and you probably have yourself. It's simply the fact that we keep coming across the little phrase 'under heaven' or 'under the sun.' Let's get down to what our 'Professor' has to say, and try to pick out the phrases 'under the sun' or 'under heaven':

> "The words of the Preacher, the son of David, king in Jerusalem. "Vanity of vanities," says the Preacher, "Vanity of vanities! All is vanity." What advantage does man have in all his work Which he does under the sun? A generation goes and a generation comes, But the earth remains forever. Also, the sun rises and the

sun sets; And hastening to its place it rises there again. Blowing toward the south, Then turning toward the north, The wind continues swirling along; And on its circular courses the wind returns. All the rivers flow into the sea, Yet the sea is not full. To the place where the rivers flow, There they flow again. All things are wearisome; Man is not able to tell it. The eye is not satisfied with seeing, Nor is the ear filled with hearing. That which has been is that which will be, And that which has been done is that which will be done. So there is nothing new under the sun.

Is there anything of which one might say, "See this, it is new"? Already it has existed for ages which were before us. There is no remembrance of earlier things; and also of the later things which will occur, there will be for them no remembrance among those who will come later still. I, the Preacher, have been king over Israel in Jerusalem. And I set my mind to seek and explore by wisdom concerning all that has been done under heaven. It is a grievous task which God has given to the sons of men to be afflicted with. I have seen all the works which have been done under the sun, and behold, all is vanity and striving after wind" (Ecclesiastes 1:1-14).

There we have it once more in that last verse, verse 14: 'under the sun.' What this is indicating to us is that 'the Professor' who is doing the research is limiting the scope of his study. He's exploring the significance of everything from the point of view of fallen humanity. Not that he's an atheist himself, of course,

3

because he sometimes refers to God in a way that would preclude that from being the case. But for the purpose of this research, he's adopting more or less an atheistic perspective: one that doesn't try to take account of God or higher things than what the eye can see. He's doing this – not to defend that viewpoint – but only to explore the best that worldview can offer as far as explaining the true meaning of life.

And, as we're going to find out, it can't offer us very much, for if atheism is true, then life is ultimately without purpose. We're jumping ahead of ourselves for a moment, but a modern 'Professor,' the Nobel prize-winning scientist, Steven Weinberg, is an outspoken atheist. He writes: 'The more the universe seems comprehensible, the more it also seems pointless. But if there is no solace in the fruits of our research, there is at least some consolation in the research itself ... The effort to understand the universe is one of the very few things that lifts human life a little above the level of farce, and gives it some of the grace of tragedy' (from *The First Three Minutes*). Weinberg considers life as being ultimately without purpose, but he does talk about how a passion for actually doing science gives life a temporary lift above the level of farce – and he finds a crumb of comfort in that. That's a remarkably similar finding, as we'll see, to what the Professor in the Bible Book of Ecclesiastes discovers through his research.

But the Bible's endorsed study cannot end on such a pessimistic note as Steven Weinberg ended his. As the writer of the Bible Book of Ecclesiastes digs away at the problem, uncovering various different strands of evidence, he digs down until in chapter 12 he hits bedrock. And that bedrock, as it were, is

4

God himself. Along the way, as we'll see, there are glimpses of a higher, divine perspective – one that is necessary in order to transcend meaninglessness. But we must be patient. The 'Professor' takes his time so that we get to feel the depressing weight of all research that doesn't have God as its starting assumption. And that's illustrated by the opinion of Steven Weinberg that we noted earlier. For he concludes that life 'under the sun' is ultimately without purpose, and that's depressingly pessimistic.

If we recall again verse 13, where the 'Professor' says: "And I set my mind to seek and explore by wisdom concerning all that has been done under heaven. It is a grievous task which God has given to the sons of men to be afflicted with." From that, we see that the Bible 'Professor' never descends into atheism himself. He even considers his research task as a God-given one. But he effectively experiments with what practical atheism has to offer as regards life's ultimate meaning and the making sense of life. His conclusion is that without God in the picture, there can be no ultimately satisfying or meaningful human existence.

In later studies, we'll see how such thoughts as whether or not we believe in justice has a bearing on this. For the 'Professor' weighed up how in this life 'under the sun' gloriously good and blatantly bad people share the same fate of death. He considers that unsatisfactory, and so the choice is between saying: 'tough, it is what it is,' or realising that there must be 'a day of reckoning' beyond this short life. He points us very clearly in the direction of the second option with the reminder that the very fact we humans search for meaning (while the animal creation doesn't) points to the imprint of God upon us, if we're willing to recognise

5

it (Ecclesiastes 3:11).

2

FUTILITY AND HOPE

Oscar Wilde, the famous Irish poet and playwright who died in 1900, once said, 'Pleasure is the only thing one should live for.' And pleasure is another topic our Bible 'Professor' researched in his quest for meaning. Before we get into that, we should link back to the fact that our previous study took us as far as verse 15 in chapter one of Ecclesiastes. That verse says: "What is crooked cannot be straightened and what is lacking cannot be counted."

And that pretty well captures the sense of futility that repeatedly comes across throughout the first chapter of this unusual Bible book. We've been thinking of it as unusual because it seems to paint a very bleak picture of life. That's because it's trying to appreciate what life looks like to someone who doesn't start out with the assumption that God exists. The researcher here does in fact believe in God's existence, but he's deliberately limiting the scope of his study to the natural world 'under the sun.' In effect, he's exploring what life looks like for an atheist. By setting aside any higher perspective, he repeatedly in this book comes to the conclusion – in fact, he's driven to it – that life in this world for anyone is an exercise in futility.

Now, within the Bible's bigger picture – and especially Romans 8 verse 20 - we know precisely why this creation was subjected to the kind of futility that frustrates the 'Professor' here. That verse, and the one that follows, from the New Testament say: "For the creation was subjected to futility, not willingly, but because of Him who subjected it, in hope that the creation itself also will be set free from its slavery to corruption into the freedom of the glory of the children of God." That's the source of the futility of which the 'Professor' here speaks. God subjected this world, this universe, to futility as a consequence of human rebellion against its creator. (This is shown to be the case if we were to read further in Paul's writings). But, thankfully, we have the added information that God subjected it in hope of liberation. Neither scientific advancement nor godless philosophy can bring about that longed for liberation, that's for sure – which, in a way, brings us back to the search for real meaning in life.

We rejoin the 'Professor' in his quest ... He begins to research different opinions. Is ultimate meaning to be found in pleasure, he asks? Today, people turn to drink and drugs. These can deliver fleeting highs. But chasing satisfaction, fulfilment and meaning in pleasure proves to be like seeing a mirage in front of us and trying to grasp it - only to find it's always retreating out of reach. We never get there. The second chapter of the Bible book of Ecclesiastes opens with the 'Professor' thinking aloud:

"I said to myself, "Come now, I will test you with

8

pleasure. So enjoy yourself." And behold, it too was futility. I said of laughter, "It is madness," and of pleasure, "What does it accomplish?" I explored with my mind how to stimulate my body with wine while my mind was guiding me wisely, and how to take hold of folly, until I could see what good there is for the sons of men to do under heaven the few years of their lives. I enlarged my works: I built houses for myself, I planted vineyards for myself; I made gardens and parks for myself and I planted in them all kinds of fruit trees; I made ponds of water for myself from which to irrigate a forest of growing trees. I bought male and female slaves and I had homeborn slaves. Also I possessed flocks and herds larger than all who preceded me in Jerusalem. Also, I collected for myself silver and gold and the treasure of kings and provinces. I provided for myself male and female singers and the pleasures of men—many concubines" (Ecclesiastes 2:1-8).

Hedonism – the unbridled pursuit of pleasure – as is well described in these Bible verses, is ultimately shown to be unsatisfactory. "Between the famous and the infamous there is but one step, if as much as one," writes Oscar Wilde in *De Profundis* (from the depths). He seemed to walk that narrow line between fame and infamy, trying to become a martyr to the gay cause, by not avoiding the libel action and conviction for gross indecency that finally undid him. The predominant theme of that particular writing of his, *De Profundis,* is the importance of sorrow as the unmatched teacher. He goes as far as saying: "Where there is sorrow there is holy ground.

9

Prosperity, pleasure and success, may be rough of grain and common in fibre, but sorrow is the most sensitive of all created things. Sorrow is where sacred truths are learned."

Malcolm Muggeridge was someone who, after failing to find satisfaction in a sensuous lifestyle, came to find satisfaction in God. Something he said fully supports what the Bible 'Professor' says: "When I look back on my life nowadays, which I sometimes do, what strikes me most forcibly about it is that what seemed at the time most significant and seductive, seems now most futile and absurd. For instance, success in all of its various guises; being known and being praised; ostensible pleasures, like acquiring money or seducing women, or traveling, going to and fro in the world and up and down in it like Satan, exploring and experiencing whatever Vanity Fair has to offer. In retrospect all these exercises in self-gratification seem pure fantasy, what Pascal called 'licking the earth.'" Muggeridge there mentions success and money, and our Bible 'Professor' turns to those in chapter 2 verses 10 and 11. He says they give a certain sense of achievement but never enough. Here's what he actually says:

> "All that my eyes desired I did not refuse them. I did not withhold my heart from any pleasure, for my heart was pleased because of all my labor and this was my reward for all my labor. Thus I considered all my activities which my hands had done and the labor which I had exerted, and behold all was vanity and striving after wind and there was no profit under the sun."

'His heart was pleased' with his work, with his achievements. He can talk about it being rewarding, but further, more prolonged reflection, ends with him dismissing it as of 'no profit.' Jack Higgens, author of successful novels, including The Eagle Has Landed, was asked what he would like to have known as a boy. Would you like to know his answer? It was: I'd have liked to have known "That when you get to the top, there's nothing there." (Our Daily Bread, July 9, 1994). In a way, his experiments have been repeated by many others in every generation surely, and down to the present day certainly.

Freddie Mercury was a British singer, lead vocalist of the rock band Queen, and regarded as one of the greatest lead singers in the history of rock music. His was a flamboyant, sensual lifestyle. Money, fame, adulation: he appeared to many of his fans to have it all, but among his lyrics are found the words: 'There must be more to life than this.' There is. The Apostle Paul says:

> "As for the rich in this present age, charge them not to be haughty, nor to set their hopes on the uncertainty of riches, but on God, who richly provides us with everything to enjoy. They are to do good, to be rich in good works, to be generous and ready to share, thus storing up treasure for themselves as a good foundation for the future, so that they may take hold of that which is truly life" (1 Timothy 6:17-19 ESV).

Those final words bear repeating: take hold of that which is truly life.' May I ask, have you done that? I hope you know God's rich provision, and are enjoying it. Let's finish with the words of Jesus Christ:

"The land of a rich man was very productive. And he began reasoning to himself, saying, 'What shall I do, since I have no place to store my crops?' Then he said, 'This is what I will do: I will tear down my barns and build larger ones, and there I will store all my grain and my goods. And I will say to my soul, "Soul, you have many goods laid up for many years to come; take your ease, eat, drink and be merry." But God said to him, 'You fool! This very night your soul is required of you; and now who will own what you have prepared?' So is the man who stores up treasure for himself, and is not rich toward God" (Luke 12:16-21).

3

THE VANISHING POINT

As we've noted previously, the Nobel prize-winning scientist Steven Weinberg was an outspoken atheist. He wrote: 'The more the universe seems comprehensible, the more it also seems pointless. But if there is no solace in the fruits of our research, there is at least some consolation in the research itself ... The effort to understand the universe is one of the very few things that lifts human life a little above the level of farce, and gives it some of the grace of tragedy' (from *The First Three Minutes*). Weinberg considers life as being ultimately without purpose, but he does talk about how a passion for actually doing science gives life a temporary lift above the level of farce – and he finds a crumb of comfort in that. In other words, Weinberg finds a crumb of comfort in the process of researching, even if the conclusion he draws from the research is that everything is meaningless.

That's a remarkably similar finding, as we'll see now, to what the 'Professor' in the Bible Book of Ecclesiastes discovers through his own research. His finding was that everything is meaningless, but you can still get a certain – albeit very limited - amount of satisfaction, and even enjoyment, from doing a job well. We might expect a Bible writer to say a lot more than that, but we need to remember that in this book, and for the purposes of research only, the writer – our 'Professor' so to speak – has artificially limited the scope of his research to being that of a purely earth-bound study. In other words, for the sake of argument, he's not allowing himself to consider the possibility that life could have a higher meaning than what might be explored in the things around us that we can see and experiment with.

Let's see what else our Bible 'Professor' says as he now turns his spotlight on to the topic of education and knowledge as we come to Ecclesiastes chapter two verses 16 to 20:

"For there is no lasting remembrance of the wise man as with the fool, inasmuch as in the coming days all will be forgotten. And how the wise man and the fool alike die! So I hated life, for the work which had been done under the sun was grievous to me; because everything is futility and striving after wind. Thus I hated all the fruit of my labor for which I had labored under the sun, for I must leave it to the man who will come after me. And who knows whether he will be a wise man or a fool? Yet he will have control over all the fruit of my labor for which I have labored by acting wisely under the sun. This too is vanity. Therefore I completely despaired of all the fruit of my labor for which I had labored under the sun" (Ecclesiastes 2:16-20).

He concludes that both the wise and foolish end up dead, which cannot be denied. Death is more certain than taxes. But the added pessimism here is that in the longer term there's no advantage in advancing your education in the short-term. For it's just as certain the wise will die as it is that the fool will die. However, having said that, the preliminary evaluation in verses 24 to 26 anticipates arguments to come. Here's what they say:

> "There is nothing better for a man than to eat and drink and tell himself that his labor is good. This also I have seen that it is from the hand of God. For who can eat and who can have enjoyment without Him? For to a person who is good in His sight He has given wisdom and knowledge and joy, while to the sinner He has given the task of gathering and collecting so that he may give to one who is good in God's sight. This too is vanity and striving after wind" (Ecclesiastes 2:24-26).

What he's discovered, as a provisional finding, is that there are certain legitimate God-given pleasures in work – as Steven Weinberg states – just as there's also enjoyment to be had in food and drink. But no great weight of significance can be laid there. Genuine pleasures from God are given to the man who pleases him. Devoid of God, however, in the final analysis, all things like this end up meaningless.

He next considers time which presents us with another indicator of meaninglessness. Births, deaths and marriages are all registered at a point in time. The rise and fall of empires get documented in history books. Events ranging from the personal to the international form the very tapestry of life, but there's something deeper in chapter 3 verse 11. There's such a thing as

God's time. Of course, it's something that any study restricted to what's 'under heaven' can't take any proper accounting of. But our researcher, the Bible 'Professor' slips us a hint here. Just as a 'leaked document' prematurely makes known what the official finding is going to tell us, that's what happens here too.

> "There is an appointed time for everything. And there is a time for every event under heaven— A time to give birth and a time to die; A time to plant and a time to uproot what is planted. A time to kill and a time to heal; A time to tear down and a time to build up. A time to weep and a time to laugh; A time to mourn and a time to dance. A time to throw stones and a time to gather stones; A time to embrace and a time to shun embracing. A time to search and a time to give up as lost; A time to keep and a time to throw away. A time to tear apart and a time to sew together; A time to be silent and a time to speak. A time to love and a time to hate; A time for war and a time for peace. What profit is there to the worker from that in which he toils? I have seen the task which God has given the sons of men with which to occupy themselves. He has made everything appropriate in its time. He has also set eternity in their heart, yet so that man will not find out the work which God has done from the beginning even to the end" (Ecclesiastes 3:1-11).

As we say, this consideration of time seemingly presents us with just another indicator of meaninglessness ... Ah, but wait! There's also such a thing as God's time. Everything is made beautiful in its time, which is God's time. At a human level,

16

there seems to be nothing but meaningless repetition and boring cycles, but seen from above it's God's providential design with a beginning and end to each section of the pattern. Unlike the brute creation, we are immersed in eternity. That's why we look for meaning whereas animals don't. Eternity, to the Hebrews, was the vanishing point of time out of mind. Earlier, we spoke of the tapestry of life. Corrie Ten Boom was someone who helped many Jews escape the Nazis from the Holocaust by hiding them in her home. She was arrested and sent to a concentration camp. She wrote this poem:

> My life is but a weaving
> Between my God and me.
> I cannot choose the colors
> He weaveth steadily.
> Oft' times He weaveth sorrow;
> And I in foolish pride
> Forget He sees the upper
> And I the underside.
> Not 'til the loom is silent
> And the shuttles cease to fly
> Will God unroll the canvas
> And reveal the reason why.
> The dark threads are as needful
> In the weaver's skillful hand
> As the threads of gold and silver
> In the pattern He has planned.

There's now a hint of sovereignty for those who can bring themselves to embrace a higher perspective than under the sun. It's true there's a time for each one of us to be born, a time for each one of us to die, but the psalmist could say in his prayer to God: 'my times are in your hand.' William Cowper, the hymnwriter, put it like this: "God moves in a mysterious way his wonders to perform ... Deep in unfathomable mines of never-failing skill, he treasures up his bright designs, and works his sov'reign will ... behind a frowning providence he hides a smiling face... God is his own interpreter, and he will make it plain." Our researcher, the Bible 'Professor' wished things could be plainer. But he was forced to the view that only in the hidden working of God could deeper, lasting meaning be found.

> "I know that there is nothing better for them than to rejoice and to do good in one's lifetime; moreover, that every man who eats and drinks sees good in all his labor—it is the gift of God. I know that everything God does will remain forever; there is nothing to add to it and there is nothing to take from it..." (Ecclesiastes 3:12–14).

Contentment comes with the conviction that only what God does remains, and nothing of our work. While the unbeliever is brought to despair; the believer is brought to faith and worship.

4

EVEN RELIGION IS FUTILE

What we've been seeing in our studies up to this point are two things. First, the doing of something can bring us enjoyment even if in the long run the result proves meaningless. Second, if we dare to allow ourselves the possibility that there could be a higher perspective, higher than is found in things 'under heaven,' then – and only then – is there any hope of ultimate meaning and only then is it possible to make sense of life. But these are asides in our Bible 'Professor's' research because although he makes these comments in passing, almost as asides, he's really intent on exploring if life can in any way give lasting satisfaction without the need to invoke God. In chapters 3 and 4, it's as if the 'Professor's' frustration builds and builds. Here are some samples:

> "Furthermore, I have seen under the sun that in the place of justice there is wickedness and in the place of righteousness there is wickedness. I said to myself, "God will judge both the righteous man and the wicked man," for a time for every matter and for every deed

is there. I said to myself concerning the sons of men, "God has surely tested them in order for them to see that they are but beasts." For the fate of the sons of men and the fate of beasts is the same. As one dies so dies the other; indeed, they all have the same breath and there is no advantage for man over beast, for all is vanity. All go to the same place. All came from the dust and all return to the dust. Who knows that the breath of man ascends upward and the breath of the beast descends downward to the earth? I have seen that nothing is better than that man should be happy in his activities, for that is his lot. For who will bring him to see what will occur after him?" (Ecclesiastes 3:16–22).

As we move into chapter 4, there's still no relief from this unrelenting pessimism:

"So I congratulated the dead who are already dead more than the living who are still living. But better off than both of them is the one who has never existed, who has never seen the evil activity that is done under the sun. I have seen that every labor and every skill which is done is the result of rivalry between a man and his neighbor. This too is vanity and striving after wind. There was a certain man without a dependent, having neither a son nor a brother, yet there was no end to all his labor. Indeed, his eyes were not satisfied with riches and he never asked, "And for whom am I laboring and depriving myself of pleasure?" This too is vanity and it is a grievous task" (Ecclesiastes

4:2-4,8).

After these declarations of futility, the 'Professor' turns his attention to explore the world of those who are religiously-minded, but who are lacking in sincerity or conviction. Recall how he's previously explored whether pleasure or education and academic study can provide sufficient meaning to help us make sense of life. He also spent time considering time itself! He was thinking about the apparent randomness with which life events are scheduled - including the senselessness, as it seems to us, of a young 'innocent' life coming prematurely to an end. Having failed to find a basis for meaning in such things, he now turns to explore the religious world. But his scepticism shines through here also in terms of exposing the insincerely pious as those who don't keep their promises and commitments.

> "Guard your steps as you go to the house of God and draw near to listen rather than to offer the sacrifice of fools; for they do not know they are doing evil. Do not be hasty in word or impulsive in thought to bring up a matter in the presence of God. For God is in heaven and you are on the earth; therefore let your words be few ... When you make a vow to God, do not be late in paying it; for He takes no delight in fools. Pay what you vow!" (Ecclesiastes 5:1-4).

When he wrote "Do not be hasty in word or impulsive in thought to bring up a matter in the presence of God," it's as if he's saying "Don't hurry your heart in God's presence." Perhaps this might translate as: 'religious observance is also meaningless if there's no awe of God.'

"If you see oppression of the poor and denial of justice and righteousness in the province, do not be shocked at the sight; for one official watches over another official, and there are higher officials over them … He who loves money will not be satisfied with money, nor he who loves abundance with its income. This too is vanity. When good things increase, those who consume them increase. So what is the advantage to their owners except to look on? The sleep of the working man is pleasant, whether he eats little or much; but the full stomach of the rich man does not allow him to sleep" (Ecclesiastes 5:8, 10-12).

He seems to be saying that officialdom is better than anarchy, but sadly corruption is endemic in many cultures. In step with popular cynicism, he says it's all the way up the food chain. Greed, however, receives its just compensation in sleepless nights.

"There is a grievous evil which I have seen under the sun: riches being hoarded by their owner to his hurt. When those riches were lost through a bad investment and he had fathered a son, then there was nothing to support him. As he had come naked from his mother's womb, so will he return as he came. He will take nothing from the fruit of his labor that he can carry in his hand. This also is a grievous evil—exactly as a man is born, thus will he die. So what is the advantage to him who toils for the wind? Furthermore, as for every man to whom God has given riches and wealth, He has also empowered him to eat from them and to

22

receive his reward and rejoice in his labor; this is the gift of God. For he will not often consider the years of his life, because God keeps him occupied with the gladness of his heart" (Ecclesiastes 5:13-16, 19-20).

First there was the extreme frustration of possessing everything – everything that is, except the capacity to enjoy it. For that elusive possession of being able to enjoy what you have is a gift from God. But why might we not be able to enjoy what we have? Reasons could include business failure; chronic illness; war; evil manipulation of someone higher; insanity: these can also be reasons why we don't possess the capacity to enjoy our work.

"There is an evil which I have seen under the sun and it is prevalent among men— a man to whom God has given riches and wealth and honor so that his soul lacks nothing of all that he desires; yet God has not empowered him to eat from them, for a foreigner enjoys them. This is vanity and a severe affliction. If a man fathers a hundred children and lives many years, however many they be, but his soul is not satisfied with good things and he does not even have a proper burial, then I say, "Better the miscarriage than he, for it comes in futility and goes into obscurity; and its name is covered in obscurity. It never sees the sun and it never knows anything; it is better off than he. Even if the other man lives a thousand years twice and does not enjoy good things—do not all go to one place?" (Ecclesiastes 6:1-6).

The stillborn, the 'Professor' says, go to the same place, and are better off, than those who have lived twice times 1000 years and fathered a hundred children! With hyperbole like this, he's really emphasizing meaninglessness, isn't he? As his following questions demonstrate:

> "For what advantage does the wise man have over the fool? What advantage does the poor man have, knowing how to walk before the living? What the eyes see is better than what the soul desires. This too is futility and a striving after wind" (Ecclesiastes 6:8-9).

What he says is like the modern expression of those who work in order to eat, and eat in order to work. Even wisdom has its downside. Not content with what we see, we desire for something beyond the material. Beautiful objects may distract us, or even content us for a while, but the experience of countless lives is that material things don't ultimately satisfy us. That's what the Rolling stones were intending to say when they mangled the grammar, and said 'I can't find no satisfaction.' Author C.S. Lewis put it in a more literary form when he said: ""Creatures are not born with desires unless satisfaction for these desires exists. A baby feels hunger; well, there is such a thing as food. ... If I find in myself a desire which no experience in this world can satisfy, the most probable explanation is that I was made for another world." (Mere Christianity, Bk. III, chap. 10, "Hope"). We would readily recognize desires we all have, such as: to be appreciated, to have happiness, to find fulfilment, but ultimately only a relationship with God offers these in fullest measure. The French philosopher effectively wrote about us all having a God-shaped hole (Blaise Pascal, *Pensées* VII(425)).

5

NOSTALGIA AIN'T WHAT IT USED TO BE

The kind of wisdom that doesn't start off by showing respect for God is a limited kind of wisdom, and as a result is quite inadequate as a vehicle for discovering the full meaning of life. That, in short, is the message of the Bible book of Ecclesiastes. The Bible, God's library of 66 books, contains a section known as Wisdom Literature. The Bible Book of Proverbs belongs to this. The proverbs we find there are pithy statements of truth, fragments of distilled wisdom. The Book we're studying, Ecclesiastes, is also found in this section but it's a most unusual entry. Its design and purpose seems to be to show the limitation of mere human wisdom. We've now arrived at chapter 7, and it tries to weigh up what's better and what's worse in life. It's as if the 'Professor' has settled for what's better – if he can't find true meaning, why not just work out the better way to get through life.

What's better in life and death (Ecclesiastes 7:1-4 NKJV)?

> "A good name is better than precious ointment,
> And the day of death than the day of one's birth;
> Better to go to the house of mourning
> Than to go to the house of feasting,
> For that is the end of all men;
> And the living will take it to heart.
> Sorrow is better than laughter,
> For by a sad countenance the heart is made better."

Chapter 7 is a string of proverbs. But these are worldly proverbs, not like the ones found in the Book of Proverbs. There's some common sense to them, so they're useful as far as they go, but they're also cynical and some are rather gloomy. Here's an example: "... the day of one's death is better than the day of one's birth."

Notice what I say about them being gloomy. This one is actually quite morbid, but according to Spurgeon, the famous preacher, "Some of the old Romish monks always read their Bibles with a candle stuck in a skull." Perhaps, this was to them a reminder of their mortality, of how we must all bring our days to an end as a tale that is told. Or, more biblically, in the prayer of Moses: "teach us to number our days, that we may gain a heart of wisdom" (Psalm 90:12). Death is said here to have some benefit, but only compared to our birth! The world-weary cynicism of the researcher simply oozes out of this. It's as if the writer has reflected on the bitter injustices of life – and all of

26

its frustrations and futility – and concluded it's better off being dead than alive. There's nothing of biblical hope in this verse. It can't begin to compare with what we find the Apostle Paul writing in Philippians chapter one verse 21: "For to me, to live is Christ and to die is gain."

What the Apostle Paul is saying is that having lived his life well in serving God, he had an assurance from the Holy Spirit that death would usher him into a sense of blessedness that far surpassed the best of what life down here had to offer. We should caution that this is a confidence that can only be enjoyed now by those who are believers on the Lord Jesus whom Paul served.

What's better in mourning and pleasure (Ecclesiastes 7:4-7)?

Let's sample a little more from the Bible 'Professor' who shares with us his research in the Book of Ecclesiastes:

> "The mind of the wise is in the house of mourning, While the mind of fools is in the house of pleasure. It is better to listen to the rebuke of a wise man Than for one to listen to the song of fools. For as the crackling of thorn bushes under a pot, So is the laughter of the fool; And this too is futility. For oppression makes a wise man mad, And a bribe corrupts the heart" (Ecclesiastes 7:4-7).

In a similar vein to death being better than birth, the 'Professor' now says mourning is more beneficial than pleasure. Gifted writers of the modern era have told us that sorrow is holy ground and that God whispers in our pleasures but shouts in our pain. And it was certainly meant to be a case of the louder the better, for it brought an acknowledgement and appreciation of the God who is truly there, and longs to communicate with us. In a similar way rebukes – if they're from a wise person – are better for us than songs – if they come from the lips of fools. This continues the theme of comparing things to assess which is better than the other. This is how he continues:

What's better in wisdom and folly (Ecclesiastes 7:5-9 NKJV)?

> "It is better to hear the rebuke of the wise
> Than for a man to hear the song of fools.
> For like the crackling of thorns under a pot,
> So is the laughter of the fool.
> This also is vanity.
> Surely oppression destroys a wise man's reason,
> And a bribe debases the heart.
> The end of a thing is better than its beginning;
> The patient in spirit is better than the proud in spirit.
> Do not hasten in your spirit to be angry,
> For anger rests in the bosom of fools."

The skilful play on words gets rather lost in translation, but one translator, Moffatt, captures it well enough: *Like nettles crackling under kettles.* Thorns were a rapidly burning, easily extinguishable fuel in the ancient world" (Eaton). "They make a great noise, a great blaze; and are extinguished in a few moments. Such indeed, comparatively, are the joys of life; they are noisy, flashy, and transitory" (Clarke). And so now, in verses 8 and 10, we come to the lines that gave rise to the heading of this study, which if I may remind you was: Nostalgia ain't what it used to be:

> "The end of a matter is better than its beginning;
> Patience of spirit is better than haughtiness of spirit.
> Do not say, 'Why is it that the former days were better than these?' For it is not from wisdom that you ask about this" (Ecclesiastes 7:8,10).

What's better in past and present (Ecclesiastes 7:10-12 NKJV)?

> "Do not say, 'Why were the former days better than these?'
> For you do not inquire wisely concerning this.
> Wisdom is good with an inheritance,
> And profitable to those who see the sun.
> For wisdom is a defense as money is a defense,
> But the excellence of knowledge is that wisdom gives life to those who have it."

Solomon understood our tendency to romanticize the past, and think it was better than our current time. He cautioned against it, for he's already declared that one age is very much like another. "What has been is what will be ... and there is nothing new under the sun" (Ecclesiastes 1:9). "Wise people certainly learn from the past, but they live in the present with all its opportunities" (Wright). Wisdom is good with an inheritance, and profitable to

29

those who see the sun: With the Professor's premise, the best kind of life is found with wisdom and money (an inheritance). This wisdom – called also excellence of knowledge – gives whatever life can be had in an *under the sun* world.

> "I have seen everything during my lifetime of futility; there is a righteous man who perishes in his righteousness and there is a wicked man who prolongs his life in his wickedness" (Ecclesiastes 7:15).

> "Behold, I have found only this, that God made men upright, but they have sought out many devices" (Ecclesiastes 7:29).

The 'Professor' concludes that wisdom gives a better perspective on life, but realizes that wisdom that doesn't start at the feet of the Lord is limited and insufficient to discover meaning. For him, life is meaningless. Remember the English bard (Shakespeare) said that life is 'a tale told by an idiot, full of sound and fury, signifying nothing.' That's the same sentiment. But we can conclude, as the 'Professor' concludes chapter 7, on a salutary but hopeful note. In the last verse we read that an understanding of the Creation, and the subsequent Fall of humanity, brings us closer to the best worldview to have. In Creation, God made us upright or having integrity, but we rebelled against his rule and have sought out many devices. This is truly the key to unlocking life's meaning!

6

WHERE'S THE JUSTICE IN INJUSTICE?

A genuine question these days is: 'Do you have any hope in the future of humankind and specifically for our generation, and if so, what?' There seems to be a mix of sorrow and pessimism in the thoughts of the enquirer. But G.K. Chesterton (As I Was Saying, Ed. Robert Knille, Grand Rapids: Eerdmans, 1985, p.267) distinguishes between sorrow and pessimism, saying there's a world of difference between sorrow and pessimism: 'Sorrow is founded on the value of *something*, and pessimism upon the value of *nothing*.' In terms of hope for the future, this makes all the difference. And in terms of the research of the Bible 'Professor' in the Book of Ecclesiastes, pessimism - as we are finding - is the order of the day. This is because the researcher has chosen to confine his study to things 'under heaven.'

A Christian apologist (Ravi Zacharias, The Logic of God, Grand Rapids: Zondervan, 2019) once had breakfast with an atheist who repeatedly insisted that there was no evidence for God. At one point, however, he did share how much he loved his wife, and painfully recounted details of her battle with disease. His wife was dying and he could do nothing. After all the intellectual arguments had run into a determined resistance, the Christian asked him why he loved his wife. The atheist just stared. "Don't you see her as a unique woman of intrinsic value to you?" he was asked. "Yes," he answered. "But how can she have such value," was the reply, "if all life is nothing more than chemicals?" That was the blow that penetrated his armour.

If we want to believe in hope for the future based on a higher perspective, then while the reality of sorrow remains, it's founded on the value of everything that has any meaning to us. On the other hand, limited to what's under the sun, there are no grounds for anything other than pessimism, for where can we find value and meaning amid recycled star stuff? The themes of sorrow and injustice surface as we arrive at chapter 8 of the Book of Ecclesiastes. To put it bluntly: 'Why do the bad have it good and the good have it bad?'

> "So then, I have seen the wicked buried, those who used to go in and out from the holy place, and they are soon forgotten in the city where they did thus. This too is futility. Because the sentence against an evil deed is not executed quickly, therefore the hearts of the sons of men among them are given fully to do evil. There is futility which is done on the earth, that is, there are righteous men to whom it happens according to the deeds of the wicked. On the other hand, there are evil men to whom it happens according to the deeds of the righteous. I say that this too is futility" (Ecclesiastes

8:10-11,14).

Why do good men and women suffer? This was the great question of the Book of Job. And surely the most poignant treatment of suffering in all the Bible is the story of Job. Job was an innocent man who suffered terribly. More than 40 chapters are devoted to the account of this one man's suffering: a good man to whom bad things happened. Are we merely dancing to our DNA? Does ruling God out of the meaning of life equation make it impossible to solve? The atheistic professor today says: "The universe that we observe has precisely the properties we should expect if there is, at bottom, no design, no purpose, no evil, no good, nothing but pitiless indifference" (*River out of Eden: A Darwinian View of Life*). That is the atheist view in a nutshell. There is no evil.

It's been said that no other single issue keeps more people from God – or troubles them so much in their relationship with God - than the issue of suffering. At 9:02, in the morning of April 19, 1995, Gulf War veteran, Timothy McVeigh detonated 4,800 lbs of fertilizer and fuel oil. The resulting blast destroyed the Federal government Building in Oklahoma, killing 168 people. That bombing was then the largest act of domestic terrorism in the U.S., shattering its pre-911 innocence. Rescue services, as well as bystanders, rushed to pull victims out of the twisted wreckage. As they sifted through the rubble, the small, half-buried body of a critically injured infant was found, and so 1-year-old (Miss) Baylee Almon was thrust into the arms of firefighter Capt. Chris Fields ... an image captured by the world's media. Baylee didn't make it, her one name out of the 168 remains with me, since she was the same age as my own son. In the vortex of pain, whether

33

our own or caught up in the observed grief of others, it seems the most natural question to ask is, Why? Why did that natural disaster happen? Why did my loved one get cancer? You've been there, and so have I, having lost my father to cancer.

Well then, is the reality of suffering - and the existence of evil - a valid argument against the existence of a good God? Let me approach this by asking you to imagine we're called out to a crime scene. A body has been found in the woods, and beside it lies an axe which has been shown to be the murder weapon. You make a mental note that the axe has been finely crafted. A tool, expertly designed for cutting down trees, has been diverted for the purpose of committing a foul deed. You think to yourself: suppose someone argues that because it's been put to evil use - because it's caused suffering - no-one could possibly exist who made it. What a nonsensical argument that would be! For it's clear the axe has a skilfully machined head, and its handle is an example of exquisite carpentry. True, it's been employed for a wrong use, but that in no way negates the fact that someone made it! That fact is established on grounds other than its use. And it's the same with the case for God. The existence - and use - of evil in the world doesn't negate the clear evidence from design, pointing to a supernatural designer (an argument the Bible endorses, see Romans 1:20).

But what then can we say about the existence of evil? Well, far from being a denial of God's existence – it, in fact, further strengthens the case for God's existence! Militant atheist Dawkins argues – and he's being logically consistent – that 'no god' means 'no evil.' But, wait a minute – how come there's widespread agreement that events like MH17 (the shooting down

34

of the Malaysian airliner over the Ukraine) are evil? But what kind of God is the God who is shown to exist – particularly if he allows evil and any suffering? Recently, a friend underwent surgery. He's suffered a lot of discomfort and pain as a result of the surgical procedures. But is he glad that he had the surgery? Yes, of course. There was a morally sufficient reason for the pain and suffering caused by the surgeon – namely, the longer-term well-being of the patient. Now, if humans – like that surgeon – can have a morally sufficient reason for causing suffering, then who can say that God can't have the same when he allows suffering?

When we think of an all-loving God, we tend to assume that he'd never have any moral reason to allow suffering. And we when try to imagine an all-powerful God, again we tend to assume that it's a no-brainer he'd want all his creatures to be robots, automatons without any choice but to do what's right. Clearly, we create the conflict we see with God being both all-loving and all-powerful by the assumptions we ourselves (wrongly) make! I'm reminded of a Church of Scotland minister who was being interviewed by a BBC News reporter on 21st December, 1988, after Pan Am Flight 103 had exploded in the sky over the Scottish town of Lockerbie. The fires were still burning when the reporter turned on the minister and *asked 'where is your God now?'* To which the unforgettably calm reply was: *'God has joined us in suffering - in the person of his son, he came as a man, Jesus Christ, and joined us in suffering.'* He did that, when 2,000 years ago, he paid the price of our freewill and spiritual rebellion on a Roman cross outside the city of Jerusalem in the turbulent Middle East.

But getting back to the text of Ecclesiastes, and the questions it raises about why bad things happen to good people; and why good things happen to bad people … it was the apparent force of these questions that made life seem meaningless to the researcher. Rather than facing up to the God question, the 'Professor' advises us to live for the moment.

> "So I commended pleasure, for there is nothing good for a man under the sun except to eat and to drink and to be merry, and this will stand by him in his toils throughout the days of his life which God has given him under the sun. When I gave my heart to know wisdom and to see the task which has been done on the earth (even though one should never sleep day or night), and I saw every work of God, I concluded that man cannot discover the work which has been done under the sun" (Ecclesiastes 8:15-17).

Perhaps that's the clearest hint yet of the conclusion that he's heading towards. Even though he commends pleasure, and says you can't beat eating, drinking and merry-making, he admits this is not the whole story. A neighbour of mine has a bumper sticker that says: 'One life, live it!' If the sky we see is our ultimate limit, then there's limited satisfaction in enjoying your work and pastimes to the maximum. They fail to bring any breakthrough discovery. Ruling God out of the meaning of life equation does make it impossible to solve.

Actually, that's why atheists resort to inventing 'the Noble Lie.' George Cornell in the Houston Post July 27, 1991 wrote an article called "Philosopher Says the World Desperately Needs a Noble

Lie." He quotes Loyal D. Rue, a professor from Luther College who says: "What I mean by the noble lie is one that deceives us, tricks us, compels us beyond self-interest, beyond ego, beyond family, nation, or race, that will deceive us into the view that our moral discourse must serve the interest not only of ourselves and each other but of those of the earth as well." This shows us just how wrong John Lennon's hit song 'Imagine' is. Better still is to look above the sun and embrace the higher – and nobler - truth.

7

MAKING THE BEST OF A BAD THING

The sceptic might say: 'Suppose I grant you that the case for intelligent design proves that there's intelligence behind the universe, but I want to be loved – and where in all this world of pain and injustice is there a scrap of evidence that the intelligence that made us belongs to a loving being?' The sceptic might even say: 'I'd rather believe I wasn't made than know I wasn't loved.' But what if we don't have to choose between the two; what if it's possible to know that we were made to be loved? It's a real issue ...

Sir David Attenborough is often asked why he doesn't give credit to a creator God for the wonderful animal design features he demonstrates on his shows. He replies: 'I tend to think instead of a parasitic worm that is boring through the eye of a boy sitting on the bank of a river in West Africa, [a worm] that's going to make him blind. 'And [then I ask them], "Are you telling me that the God you believe in, who you also say is an all-merciful God, who cares for each one of us individually, are you saying that God created this worm that can live in no other way than in an innocent child's eyeball? Because that doesn't seem to me to coincide with a God who's full of mercy."' He's running from the truth of God because he doesn't see the loving hand of the creator.

Actually, I'm told his response is not entirely accurate in saying that the parasitic worm can live in no other way, but leaving that lesser point aside let's deal with his main objection. The very first chapter of Genesis concludes by saying that after God had finished creating, everything was 'very good' – which can only mean that situations such as Attenborough describes – about the parasitic worm etc. - are not of God's making, but rather they arise out of how we've degraded God's purpose.

Of course, we might not want to face up to that responsibility, and prefer to put the blame on God. If so, the logical consequence is as given vent to by [Stephen] Fry when interviewed on The Meaning of Life TV programme and asked what he would say to God if he had a chance: "I'd say 'Bone cancer in children, what's that about?' How dare you create a world in which there is such misery that is not our fault," Fry replied. "It's not right. It's utterly, utterly evil. Why should I respect a capricious, mean-minded, stupid god who creates a world which is so full of injustice and pain?"

Don't you get the sense that he actually must believe in God, because that's who he's shaking his fist at? Stephen Fry would appear to be expressing moral outrage. It's fair to ask where does that sense of morality come from (distorted as it is in his case)? The best answer is that it comes from the God who's revealed in the Bible. Fry arrives at a distorted morality by suppressing the truth of the Bible's first pages and the worldview they offer us. In that worldview, God is very far from being the author of pain or the architect of disease and death. Instead, the finger is left pointing back at us: we are the architects of our own downfall, for it was we who rebelled. But all isn't lost if we follow through on the biblical remedy for the human problem.

Now, these men just mentioned represent the sceptic's position. And, in the Book of Ecclesiastes, the researcher, whom we are dubbing as the Bible 'Professor' is simulating the sceptic – but only for the purpose of his research. He's demonstrating in this powerful literary device that we search in vain for answers 'under the sun' or, in other words, we won't discover the truth about reality by coming at things from a purely secular perspective. What's more, it's as if he, too, longs to be sure of being loved ...

> "For I have taken all this to my heart and explain it that righteous men, wise men, and their deeds are in the hand of God. Man does not know whether it will be love or hatred; anything awaits him" (Ecclesiastes 9:1).

You hear the heart's hunger for being loved? The righteous and the wise and their works are in the hand of God. All things come alike to all: with his *under the sun* premise – excluding any sense of eternity or accountability in a life to come – a man or woman can be sure of neither love nor hatred in what lies before them. Creation can tell us God is; but it doesn't tell us so clearly that God loves us. And I think it's important to accept that we shouldn't measure God's love by what happens in life.

We measure God's love by what Jesus did at the cross.

On September 11, 2001, 19 militants associated with the Islamic extremist group al Qaeda hijacked four airplanes and carried out suicide attacks against targets in the United States. Two of the planes were flown into the twin towers of the World Trade Center in New York City. When the planes hit the Twin Towers, as far as I know none of the phone calls from the people on board were messages of hate or revenge - they were all messages of love – messages to their loved ones. But, horribly, an act of hatred ended their lives on that clear, sunny day in late summer. We've read: man does not know whether it will be love or hatred; anything awaits him. All kinds of people were on those planes ...

> "It is the same for all. There is one fate for the righteous and for the wicked; for the good, for the clean and for the unclean; for the man who offers a sacrifice and for the one who does not sacrifice. As the good man is, so is the sinner; as the swearer is, so is the one who is afraid to swear. This is an evil in all that is done under the sun, that there is one fate for all men. Furthermore, the hearts of the sons of men are full of evil and insanity is in their hearts throughout their lives. Afterwards they go to the dead. For whoever is joined with all the living, there is hope; surely a live dog is better than a dead lion. For the living know they will die; but the dead do not know anything, nor have they any longer a reward, for their memory is forgotten.

Indeed their love, their hate and their zeal have already

perished, and they will no longer have a share in all that is done under the sun. Go then, eat your bread in happiness and drink your wine with a cheerful heart; for God has already approved your works. Let your clothes be white all the time, and let not oil be lacking on your head. Enjoy life with the woman whom you love all the days of your fleeting life which He has given to you under the sun; for this is your reward in life and in your toil in which you have labored under the sun. Whatever your hand finds to do, do it with all your might; for there is no activity or planning or knowledge or wisdom in Sheol where you are going" (Ecclesiastes 9:1-10).

Did you hear him? He's saying that we all face death. Those verses take us through a minimalist view of life that reasons like this: life is better than death, so just try to optimize what you've got. The Professor's analysis boils down to: 'Life is utterly meaningless and our common death and destiny prove it to be so. So forget about all I have said and have a good time.' It is small hope given to despairing men and women, but it is the best he can do. It reminds me of the modern militant atheist's slogan: 'There's probably no God. Now stop worrying and enjoy your life.'

"I again saw under the sun that the race is not to the swift and the battle is not to the warriors, and neither is bread to the wise nor wealth to the discerning nor favor to men of ability; for time and chance overtake them all. Moreover, man does not know his time: like fish caught in a treacherous net and birds trapped in a

42

snare, so the sons of men are ensnared at an evil time when it suddenly falls on them" (Ecclesiastes 9:11-12).

We all face time and chance. And within a worldview of time and chance, there's nothing but blind, pitiless indifference. The best sense the sceptic can make of life from his earthbound point of view is: all is randomness, so don't think too much. If all existence and consciousness ends with death, then the *only* thing that matters is this present life (and therefore nothing really matters).

> "Also this I came to see as wisdom under the sun, and it impressed me. There was a small city with few men in it and a great king came to it, surrounded it and constructed large siegeworks against it. But there was found in it a poor wise man and he delivered the city by his wisdom. Yet no one remembered that poor man. So I said, "Wisdom is better than strength." But the wisdom of the poor man is despised and his words are not heeded. The words of the wise heard in quietness are better than the shouting of a ruler among fools. Wisdom is better than weapons of war, but one sinner destroys much good" (Ecclesiastes 9:13-18).

Establishing things by wisdom is much more difficult than destroying them by the work of even one sinner. "Adam's sin infected the whole race of man; Achan's transgression caused Israel's defeat (Joshua 7:11-12); Rehoboam's folly occasioned the great schism (1 Kings 12:16)" (Deane). Dead flies spoil a fine ointment and cause it to smell, even so just a moment's folly ruins the lifelong reputation of someone regarded as wise and honourable.

8

GROWING OLD IS NO JOKE!

The Bible 'Professor' sums up and presents his research findings with a call to remember. Before we get into what he says, I'd like us to remember some often-quoted words of Jesus Christ. We're going to discover they deliver the same message as that of the Old Testament 'Professor' in the perhaps somewhat disconcerting Book of Ecclesiastes.

> "Then the Pharisees went and plotted together how they might trap Him in what He said. And they sent their disciples to Him, along with the Herodians, saying, "Teacher, we know that You are truthful and teach the way of God in truth, and defer to no one; for You are not partial to any" (Matthew 22:15-16).

Wait a moment. That's a lot of build-up, a lot of flattery. If what comes next seems like a simple question, we can be sure it's not. It's a loaded question, coming on the heels of some plotting as to how Jesus could be trapped in his speech. I once heard a speaker

(Michael Ramsden) say that to give the right answer to a wrong question, is in fact the wrong answer. The better strategy is to discern and even expose the subtlety in the questioner's mind – or it may just be confusion. But first, what was the question that Jesus was asked?

> "'Tell us then, what do You think? Is it lawful to give a poll-tax to Caesar, or not?' But Jesus perceived their malice, and said, 'Why are you testing Me, you hypocrites? Show Me the coin used for the poll-tax.' And they brought Him a denarius. And He said to them, 'Whose likeness and inscription is this?' They said to Him, 'Caesar's.' Then He said to them, 'Then render to Caesar the things that are Caesar's; and to God the things that are God's'" (Matthew 22:17-21).

It was a straightforward question if it had come from honest hearts. But it had not. A trap was sprung in that question. If Jesus had said 'yes,' then Jewish 'purists' would have accused him of moral compromise with the power of Rome that was oppressing the nation of Israel at that time. However, if Jesus had said 'no,' then they would have reason to hand him over to the Roman authorities for non-compliance. Jesus gave neither answer, in perfect wisdom, that saw through their deceit, he asked to be shown a coin. 'Whose image is on it?,' he asked. 'Caesar's,' they replied. 'Then give to Caesar what belongs to Caesar,' before adding 'and give to God what belongs to God.' That silenced them.

But what if they had asked – as they might well have done had they been even a little sincere – 'What belongs to God?' I tend to agree with the person who suggested that Jesus may then have said: 'Whose image is on you?' Allow me to explain the force of that. For earlier in our studies in Ecclesiastes, we've heard the 'Professor' say that God made humanity with perfect integrity or 'upright' (7:29) as in God's own image and likeness, with a sense of eternity in our hearts as a clue to our origins (3:11). If the coin bearing the image of Caesar belongs to Caesar; then we who are in the image of God, belong to God. This is, in fact, the conclusion the Bible 'Professor' of the Book of Ecclesiastes reaches at the end of the twelfth chapter: that the whole duty of each one of us is to reverence God (12:13).

But let's return to see how he finally arrives at that point. Chapter ten of the book is for the most part a further reflection (almost as a parenthesis) on wisdom and folly, noting that wisdom has the advantage of giving success (10:10). Let me pause to note that in verse 19, it says: "money is the answer to everything." You would hardly think you'd find a statement like that in the Bible! This is a classic example of the danger in taking a verse out of its context, as can cruelly be done to any politician if the recording of his speech is maliciously edited. When we understand that this Bible book has set out to demonstrate the futility of any earth-bound search for ultimate meaning in life, then we can better understand why that verse is there. Those who deny God may at times think money is the answer to life's problems, but it isn't.

After that, chapters 11 and 12 reach a positive conclusion considering all the morally ambiguous happenings that have been reviewed. They begin by hinting at the need to invest in the future. We're to refuse to live just for today and instead invest

47

in the future (11:1-6). There's also the advice to live gratefully and joyfully with whatever gifts we have received (7-10). This culminates in a whole of life review. That's a very valuable thing. Today, it's as if society is tempting us to buy into the image of trying to stay 'forever young,' as Bob Dylan coined it. Think of all the products for hair colour and regeneration; creams for 'young-looking' skin; supplements to bring back 'youthful vitality,' and so on. Celebrities are paraded before us with age-defying make-up that creates the illusion we can all go on and on looking great. It's an illusion, of course, but so popular among people who don't believe in any future life - why wouldn't they try to hold on to the best years of this life? With all this in view, the closing words of chapter 11 are a dose of sanity:

> "Indeed, if a man should live many years, let him rejoice in them all, and let him remember the days of darkness, for they will be many. Everything that is to come will be futility. Rejoice, young man, during your childhood, and let your heart be pleasant during the days of young manhood ... So, remove grief and anger from your heart and put away pain from your body, because childhood and the prime of life are fleeting" (Ecclesiastes 11:8-10).

Following on from that, chapter 12 is about counselling us to be godly from youth, knowing that God brings everything into judgment. Before we hear from the 'Professor' for the last time, we're going to hear him say 'Remember.' It's as well to be aware, that 'to remember God' is not simply to recall the bare fact of his existence, but it's about acknowledging our need to abandon our presumed independence of God, and to give God his rightful

48

place. For only then can things begin to make any sense. God alone sees and gives the complete picture. Now contrary to the forever young illusion we've mentioned, there now follows right at the end of this intriguing book, a most poetic, realistic and potentially humorous account of the effects of getting older.

> "Remember also your Creator in the days of your youth, before the evil days come and the years draw near when you will say, "I have no delight in them"; before the sun and the light, the moon and the stars are darkened, and clouds return after the rain; in the day that the watchmen of the house tremble, and mighty men stoop, the grinding ones stand idle because they are few, and those who look through windows grow dim ..." (Ecclesiastes 12:1-3)

As we age, there can develop a tendency for certain conditions in which our arms experience involuntary shaking, often our back and lower limbs are not as ramrod straight as they were before, and our 'grinding ones' – namely our teeth – become few, and perhaps the dimming of sight with cataracts is intended ...

> "... and the doors on the street are shut as the sound of the grinding mill is low, and one will arise at the sound of the bird, and all the daughters of song will sing softly" (Ecclesiastes 12:4).

Difficulties of digestion, the tendency to be easily startled, as well as the deterioration of hearing (which explains why the daughters of song sing but softly) are now pinpointed.

"Furthermore, men are afraid of a high place and of terrors on the road; the almond tree blossoms, the grasshopper drags himself along, and the caperberry is ineffective. For man goes to his eternal home while mourners go about in the street" (Ecclesiastes 12:5).

In old age, we tend to be more afraid of heights and as we become less sure-footed, afraid also of being jostled in the streets. The almond tree is one that turns white with blossom just as our hair turns white with age. And with arthritis we become as those who hobble like the ungainly grasshopper. When I suggested humour before, I'd have to say it's a wry humour at best, for we wouldn't suggest for a moment there's anything amusing about the pain experienced by those suffering from arthritis.

"Remember Him before the silver cord is broken and the golden bowl is crushed, the pitcher by the well is shattered and the wheel at the cistern is crushed ..." (Ecclesiastes 12:6).

The silver cord is perhaps the spinal cord column, the golden bowl is the skull, and the pitcher and wheel could be the heart and our circulatory system. I do recall these words being spoken at my father's funeral, although the preacher's intention was to compare 'the pitcher by the well' to my father's habitual nearness to his Bible, and his resource in God. Now follow words even more commonly associated with funerals ...

"then the dust will return to the earth as it was, and the spirit will return to God who gave it. "Vanity of vanities," says the Preacher, "all is vanity!" (Ecclesi-

50

astes 12:7–8).

Now it only remains for us to state the 'Professor's' conclusion – and here he hits bedrock:

> "The conclusion, when all has been heard, is: fear God and keep His commandments, because this applies to every person. For God will bring every act to judgment, everything which is hidden, whether it is good or evil" (Ecclesiastes 12:13–14).

MORE BOOKS BY THE AUTHOR

MINDFULNESS THAT JESUS ENDORSES

Mindfulness is the trendy meditation offshoot recently endorsed by everyone from National Health Service departments in the UK to Oprah Winfrey in the US. In view of its possible Buddhist origins and the danger of becoming self-absorbed, is there a such a thing as a Biblical Mindfulness that Jesus could endorse? That's the question that Brian answers as he re-introduces us to the transforming power of biblical meditation which, instead of emptying the mind, fills it with a sense of the presence and immediacy of God, and His relevance to what we're experiencing at any moment.

MINOR PROPHETS? MAJOR ISSUES!

The so-called "Minor Prophets" of the Old Testament, such as Nahum, Micah and Malachi, are often overlooked because of their brevity and also because they might seem irrelevant to Christians of today. Brian shows how inaccurate this perception is by pointing out that each prophet not only had vital things to say to the peoples of that era, but they also raise very major issues that are absolutely relevant to believers today. Such issues include: injustice, suffering, unfaithfulness, abandonment, corruption, compassion, arrogance and wrong priorities.

IF ATHEISM IS TRUE…: THE FUTILE FAITH AND HOPELESS HYPOTHESES OF DAWKINS AND CO.

A former nuclear scientist turned missionary, Brian draws together some of his previously published writings on apologetics to produce a concerted offensive against what the apostle Paul would surely describe as the 'indefensible' arguments of the so-called 'New Atheists'. The short chapters in Brian's conversational style serve as an ideal entry-level primer for anyone wanting to get to grips with one of the most important of today's debates.

HEALTHY CHURCHES: GOD'S BIBLE BLUEPRINT FOR GROWTH

As Brian notes in the opening chapters of this book, many churches in the Western world seem to be declining in numbers and spiritual vitality. He explores some of the root causes and also how this trend could be reversed. The good news, as Brian reminds us, is that God gives us the growth blueprint in His Word through a number of key Bible words, such as sowing, reaping, planting, watering, cultivating, building and edifying. Find out the importance of each step in the process and get inspired to go for growth with, in and through, God!

TAKE YOUR MARK'S GOSPEL!

As Brian explains, Mark's Gospel answers the two most important questions that can engage the human mind - who is Jesus is and why did he die? That makes it essential reading for us all - and this accessible commentary unpacks all the key elements as well as providing study questions after each chapter for individual or group study.

ONCE SAVED, ALWAYS SAVED? THE REALITY OF ETERNAL SECURITY

The issue of whether a "born-again" Christian can lose their salvation is an absolutely critical one and has been a controversial topic amongst Christians for centuries. Brian provides a number of faith lessons which include insightful illustrations and Biblical references that all Christians can use to reassure themselves that there is no basis in the Bible for the so-called "Falling Away Doctrine". "For by grace are you saved, through faith."

GET REAL: LIVING EVERY DAY AS AN AUTHENTIC FOLLOWER OF CHRIST

Do you ever feel like you're just playing at being a Christian? Perhaps you even feel a bit of a fake or even a hypocrite - but you don't know what to change or how to change it. Here is some helpful, practical and scriptural guidance on Bible study, personal and collective prayer, worship, church life and family life, with the goal of us becoming authentic, credible disciples who live with real integrity!

ABOUT THE AUTHOR

Born and educated in Scotland, Brian worked as a government scientist until God called him into full-time Christian ministry on behalf of the Churches of God (www.churchesofgod.info). His voice has been heard on Search For Truth radio broadcasts for over 30 years (visit www.searchfortruth.podbean.com) during which time he has been an itinerant Bible teacher throughout the UK. His evangelical and missionary work outside the UK is primarily in Belgium, The Philippines and South East Central Africa. He is married to Rosemary, with a son and daughter.

ABOUT THE PUBLISHER

Hayes Press (www.hayespress.org) is a registered charity in the United Kingdom, whose primary mission is to disseminate the Word of God, mainly through literature. It is one of the largest distributors of gospel tracts and leaflets in the United Kingdom, with over 100 titles and many thousands dispatched annually. In addition to paperbacks and eBooks, Hayes Press also publishes Plus Eagles' Wings, a fun and educational Bible magazine for children, and Golden Bells, a popular daily Bible reading calendar in wall or desk formats.